BLOG PL

Copyright © 2019 by Laura Goodsell
All rights reserved. This book or any portion thereof
may not be reproduced or used in any manner whatsoever
without the express written permission of the publisher
except for the use of brief quotations in a book review.

First Printing, 2019

ISBN 9781693531293

www.AnchorOnline.co.uk

Laura@AnchorOnline.co.uk

BLOG PLANNER

Welcome to the Blog Planner, you will find 53 sections to plan out, write and organise your posts.

Writing a blog can really benefit your business, it shows you are knowledgeable in your field and readers can get to know you. As we all know people buy from people, so it's important when you write your posts to write them as if you are talking to someone and not formal and business like.

Are you stuck for topics to write about?

The best way to overcome this is to create a spiders web diagram, start by adding your main business in the middle of a large page, then around that write in the smaller topics that relate, then in each one of them break it down to smaller topics, keep going until you can't think of anymore, there you go, you now have a page full of topics to write about.

Here is an example of one I might do for my web design business, I have followed Security as a topic and have four smaller topics I can now write about or break down even further.

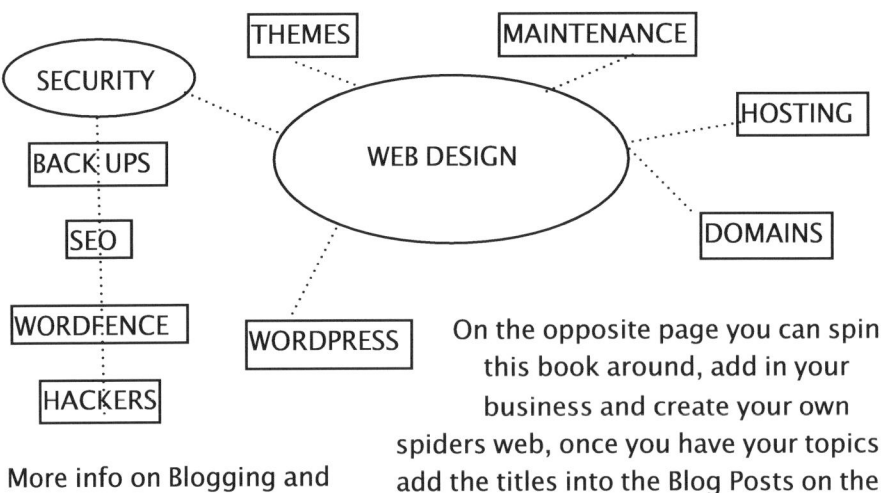

```
         THEMES         MAINTENANCE
SECURITY                        
                                HOSTING
BACK UPS      WEB DESIGN
                                DOMAINS
SEO

WORDFENCE    WORDPRESS
HACKERS
```

More info on Blogging and step by steps on publishing your posts to your WordPress account can be found on my website
www.anchoronline.co.uk

On the opposite page you can spin this book around, add in your business and create your own spiders web, once you have your topics add the titles into the Blog Posts on the following pages, you can then start planning out your content for each post, before you know it you will have a year's worth of posts ready to publish.
Great Job x

BLOG PLANNER

BLOG PLANNER

BLOG POST 1

Blog post topic
Purpose of post
Post title ideas
Key points to include

Words and phrases to use	Keywords and Tags
Workflow Write your post on your platform Insert your links Check your spelling Insert images Add in categories and Tags Add META description and keywords Publish your post Promote on social media	Images to use
	Publish date

BLOG PLANNER

Section 1

Section 2

Section 3

Final paragraph or call to action

BLOG PLANNER

BLOG POST 2

Blog post topic
Purpose of post
Post title ideas
Key points to include

Words and phrases to use	Keywords and Tags
Workflow Write your post on your platform Insert your links Check your spelling Insert images Add in categories and Tags Add META description and keywords Publish your post Promote on social media	Images to use
	Publish date

BLOG PLANNER

Section 1

Section 2

Section 3

Final paragraph or call to action

BLOG PLANNER

BLOG POST 3

Blog post topic
Purpose of post
Post title ideas
Key points to include

Words and phrases to use	Keywords and Tags
Workflow Write your post on your platform Insert your links Check your spelling Insert images Add in categories and Tags Add META description and keywords Publish your post Promote on social media	Images to use
	Publish date

BLOG PLANNER

Section 1

Section 2

Section 3

Final paragraph or call to action

BLOG PLANNER

BLOG POST 4

Blog post topic
Purpose of post
Post title ideas
Key points to include

Words and phrases to use	Keywords and Tags
Workflow Write your post on your platform Insert your links Check your spelling Insert images Add in categories and Tags Add META description and keywords Publish your post Promote on social media	**Images to use**
	Publish date

BLOG PLANNER

Section 1

Section 2

Section 3

Final paragraph or call to action

BLOG PLANNER

BLOG POST 5

Blog post topic
Purpose of post
Post title ideas
Key points to include

Words and phrases to use	Keywords and Tags
Workflow Write your post on your platform Insert your links Check your spelling Insert images Add in categories and Tags Add META description and keywords Publish your post Promote on social media	Images to use
	Publish date

BLOG PLANNER

Section 1

Section 2

Section 3

Final paragraph or call to action

BLOG PLANNER

BLOG POST 6

Blog post topic
Purpose of post
Post title ideas
Key points to include

Words and phrases to use	Keywords and Tags
Workflow Write your post on your platform Insert your links Check your spelling Insert images Add in categories and Tags Add META description and keywords Publish your post Promote on social media	**Images to use**
	Publish date

BLOG PLANNER

Section 1

Section 2

Section 3

Final paragraph or call to action

BLOG PLANNER

BLOG POST 7

Blog post topic
Purpose of post
Post title ideas
Key points to include

Words and phrases to use	Keywords and Tags
Workflow Write your post on your platform Insert your links Check your spelling Insert images Add in categories and Tags Add META description and keywords Publish your post Promote on social media	Images to use
	Publish date

BLOG PLANNER

Section 1

Section 2

Section 3

Final paragraph or call to action

BLOG PLANNER

BLOG POST 8

Blog post topic
Purpose of post
Post title ideas
Key points to include

Words and phrases to use	Keywords and Tags
Workflow Write your post on your platform Insert your links Check your spelling Insert images Add in categories and Tags Add META description and keywords Publish your post Promote on social media	Images to use
	Publish date

BLOG PLANNER

Section 1

Section 2

Section 3

Final paragraph or call to action

BLOG PLANNER

BLOG POST 9

Blog post topic
Purpose of post
Post title ideas
Key points to include

Words and phrases to use	Keywords and Tags
Workflow Write your post on your platform Insert your links Check your spelling Insert images Add in categories and Tags Add META description and keywords Publish your post Promote on social media	Images to use
	Publish date

BLOG PLANNER

Section 1

Section 2

Section 3

Final paragraph or call to action

BLOG PLANNER

BLOG POST 10

Blog post topic
Purpose of post
Post title ideas
Key points to include

Words and phrases to use	Keywords and Tags
Workflow Write your post on your platform Insert your links Check your spelling Insert images Add in categories and Tags Add META description and keywords Publish your post Promote on social media	Images to use
	Publish date

BLOG PLANNER

Section 1

Section 2

Section 3

Final paragraph or call to action

BLOG PLANNER

BLOG POST 11

Blog post topic
Purpose of post
Post title ideas
Key points to include

Words and phrases to use	Keywords and Tags
Workflow Write your post on your platform Insert your links Check your spelling Insert images Add in categories and Tags Add META description and keywords Publish your post Promote on social media	Images to use
	Publish date

BLOG PLANNER

Section 1

Section 2

Section 3

Final paragraph or call to action

BLOG PLANNER

BLOG POST 12

Blog post topic
Purpose of post
Post title ideas
Key points to include

Words and phrases to use	Keywords and Tags
Workflow Write your post on your platform Insert your links Check your spelling Insert images Add in categories and Tags Add META description and keywords Publish your post Promote on social media	Images to use
	Publish date

BLOG PLANNER

Section 1

Section 2

Section 3

Final paragraph or call to action

BLOG PLANNER

BLOG POST 13

Blog post topic
Purpose of post
Post title ideas
Key points to include

Words and phrases to use	Keywords and Tags
Workflow Write your post on your platform Insert your links Check your spelling Insert images Add in categories and Tags Add META description and keywords Publish your post Promote on social media	Images to use
	Publish date

www.AnchorOnline.co.uk

BLOG PLANNER

Section 1

Section 2

Section 3

Final paragraph or call to action

BLOG PLANNER

BLOG POST 14

Blog post topic
Purpose of post
Post title ideas
Key points to include

Words and phrases to use	Keywords and Tags
Workflow Write your post on your platform Insert your links Check your spelling Insert images Add in categories and Tags Add META description and keywords Publish your post Promote on social media	Images to use
	Publish date

BLOG PLANNER

Section 1

Section 2

Section 3

Final paragraph or call to action

BLOG PLANNER

BLOG POST 15

Blog post topic
Purpose of post
Post title ideas
Key points to include

Words and phrases to use	Keywords and Tags
Workflow Write your post on your platform Insert your links Check your spelling Insert images Add in categories and Tags Add META description and keywords Publish your post Promote on social media	Images to use
	Publish date

BLOG PLANNER

Section 1

Section 2

Section 3

Final paragraph or call to action

BLOG PLANNER

BLOG POST 16

Blog post topic
Purpose of post
Post title ideas
Key points to include

Words and phrases to use	Keywords and Tags
Workflow Write your post on your platform Insert your links Check your spelling Insert images Add in categories and Tags Add META description and keywords Publish your post Promote on social media	Images to use
	Publish date

BLOG PLANNER

Section 1

Section 2

Section 3

Final paragraph or call to action

BLOG PLANNER

BLOG POST 17

Blog post topic
Purpose of post
Post title ideas
Key points to include

Words and phrases to use	Keywords and Tags
Workflow Write your post on your platform Insert your links Check your spelling Insert images Add in categories and Tags Add META description and keywords Publish your post Promote on social media	Images to use
	Publish date

BLOG PLANNER

Section 1

Section 2

Section 3

Final paragraph or call to action

BLOG PLANNER

BLOG POST 18

Blog post topic
Purpose of post
Post title ideas
Key points to include

Words and phrases to use	Keywords and Tags
Workflow Write your post on your platform Insert your links Check your spelling Insert images Add in categories and Tags Add META description and keywords Publish your post Promote on social media	**Images to use**
	Publish date

BLOG PLANNER

Section 1

Section 2

Section 3

Final paragraph or call to action

BLOG PLANNER

BLOG POST 19

Blog post topic
Purpose of post
Post title ideas
Key points to include

Words and phrases to use	Keywords and Tags
Workflow Write your post on your platform Insert your links Check your spelling Insert images Add in categories and Tags Add META description and keywords Publish your post Promote on social media	Images to use
	Publish date

BLOG PLANNER

Section 1

Section 2

Section 3

Final paragraph or call to action

BLOG PLANNER

BLOG POST 20

Blog post topic
Purpose of post
Post title ideas
Key points to include

Words and phrases to use	Keywords and Tags
Workflow Write your post on your platform Insert your links Check your spelling Insert images Add in categories and Tags Add META description and keywords Publish your post Promote on social media	Images to use
	Publish date

BLOG PLANNER

Section 1

Section 2

Section 3

Final paragraph or call to action

BLOG PLANNER

BLOG POST 21

Blog post topic
Purpose of post
Post title ideas
Key points to include

Words and phrases to use	Keywords and Tags
Workflow Write your post on your platform Insert your links Check your spelling Insert images Add in categories and Tags Add META description and keywords Publish your post Promote on social media	**Images to use**
	Publish date

BLOG PLANNER

Section 1

Section 2

Section 3

Final paragraph or call to action

BLOG PLANNER

BLOG POST 22

Blog post topic
Purpose of post
Post title ideas
Key points to include

Words and phrases to use	Keywords and Tags
Workflow Write your post on your platform Insert your links Check your spelling Insert images Add in categories and Tags Add META description and keywords Publish your post Promote on social media	Images to use
	Publish date

BLOG PLANNER

Section 1

Section 2

Section 3

Final paragraph or call to action

BLOG PLANNER

BLOG POST 23

Blog post topic
Purpose of post
Post title ideas
Key points to include

Words and phrases to use	Keywords and Tags
Workflow Write your post on your platform Insert your links Check your spelling Insert images Add in categories and Tags Add META description and keywords Publish your post Promote on social media	Images to use
	Publish date

BLOG PLANNER

Section 1

Section 2

Section 3

Final paragraph or call to action

BLOG PLANNER

BLOG POST 24

Blog post topic
Purpose of post
Post title ideas
Key points to include

Words and phrases to use	Keywords and Tags
Workflow Write your post on your platform Insert your links Check your spelling Insert images Add in categories and Tags Add META description and keywords Publish your post Promote on social media	Images to use
	Publish date

BLOG PLANNER

Section 1

Section 2

Section 3

Final paragraph or call to action

BLOG PLANNER

BLOG POST 25

Blog post topic
Purpose of post
Post title ideas
Key points to include

Words and phrases to use	Keywords and Tags
Workflow Write your post on your platform Insert your links Check your spelling Insert images Add in categories and Tags Add META description and keywords Publish your post Promote on social media	Images to use
	Publish date

BLOG PLANNER

Section 1

Section 2

Section 3

Final paragraph or call to action

BLOG PLANNER

BLOG POST 26

Blog post topic
Purpose of post
Post title ideas
Key points to include

Words and phrases to use	Keywords and Tags
Workflow Write your post on your platform Insert your links Check your spelling Insert images Add in categories and Tags Add META description and keywords Publish your post Promote on social media	Images to use
	Publish date

BLOG PLANNER

Section 1

Section 2

Section 3

Final paragraph or call to action

BLOG PLANNER

BLOG POST 27

Blog post topic
Purpose of post
Post title ideas
Key points to include

Words and phrases to use	Keywords and Tags
Workflow Write your post on your platform Insert your links Check your spelling Insert images Add in categories and Tags Add META description and keywords Publish your post Promote on social media	Images to use
	Publish date

BLOG PLANNER

Section 1

Section 2

Section 3

Final paragraph or call to action

BLOG PLANNER

BLOG POST 28

Blog post topic
Purpose of post
Post title ideas
Key points to include

Words and phrases to use	Keywords and Tags
Workflow Write your post on your platform Insert your links Check your spelling Insert images Add in categories and Tags Add META description and keywords Publish your post Promote on social media	Images to use
	Publish date

www.AnchorOnline.co.uk

BLOG PLANNER

Section 1

Section 2

Section 3

Final paragraph or call to action

BLOG PLANNER

BLOG POST 29

Blog post topic
Purpose of post
Post title ideas
Key points to include

Words and phrases to use	Keywords and Tags
Workflow Write your post on your platform Insert your links Check your spelling Insert images Add in categories and Tags Add META description and keywords Publish your post Promote on social media	Images to use
	Publish date

BLOG PLANNER

Section 1

Section 2

Section 3

Final paragraph or call to action

BLOG PLANNER

BLOG POST 30

Blog post topic
Purpose of post
Post title ideas
Key points to include

Words and phrases to use	Keywords and Tags
Workflow Write your post on your platform Insert your links Check your spelling Insert images Add in categories and Tags Add META description and keywords Publish your post Promote on social media	Images to use
	Publish date

BLOG PLANNER

Section 1

Section 2

Section 3

Final paragraph or call to action

BLOG PLANNER

BLOG POST 31

Blog post topic
Purpose of post
Post title ideas
Key points to include

Words and phrases to use	Keywords and Tags
Workflow Write your post on your platform Insert your links Check your spelling Insert images Add in categories and Tags Add META description and keywords Publish your post Promote on social media	Images to use
	Publish date

BLOG PLANNER

Section 1

Section 2

Section 3

Final paragraph or call to action

BLOG PLANNER

BLOG POST 32

Blog post topic
Purpose of post
Post title ideas
Key points to include

Words and phrases to use	Keywords and Tags
Workflow Write your post on your platform Insert your links Check your spelling Insert images Add in categories and Tags Add META description and keywords Publish your post Promote on social media	Images to use
	Publish date

BLOG PLANNER

Section 1

Section 2

Section 3

Final paragraph or call to action

BLOG PLANNER

BLOG POST 33

Blog post topic
Purpose of post
Post title ideas
Key points to include

Words and phrases to use	Keywords and Tags
Workflow Write your post on your platform Insert your links Check your spelling Insert images Add in categories and Tags Add META description and keywords Publish your post Promote on social media	Images to use
	Publish date

BLOG PLANNER

Section 1

Section 2

Section 3

Final paragraph or call to action

BLOG PLANNER

BLOG POST 34

Blog post topic	
Purpose of post	
Post title ideas	
Key points to include	

Words and phrases to use	Keywords and Tags
Workflow Write your post on your platform Insert your links Check your spelling Insert images Add in categories and Tags Add META description and keywords Publish your post Promote on social media	Images to use
	Publish date

BLOG PLANNER

Section 1

Section 2

Section 3

Final paragraph or call to action

BLOG PLANNER

BLOG POST 35

Blog post topic
Purpose of post
Post title ideas
Key points to include

Words and phrases to use	Keywords and Tags
Workflow Write your post on your platform Insert your links Check your spelling Insert images Add in categories and Tags Add META description and keywords Publish your post Promote on social media	Images to use
	Publish date

BLOG PLANNER

Section 1

Section 2

Section 3

Final paragraph or call to action

BLOG PLANNER

BLOG POST 36

Blog post topic
Purpose of post
Post title ideas
Key points to include

Words and phrases to use	Keywords and Tags
Workflow Write your post on your platform Insert your links Check your spelling Insert images Add in categories and Tags Add META description and keywords Publish your post Promote on social media	Images to use
	Publish date

BLOG PLANNER

Section 1

Section 2

Section 3

Final paragraph or call to action

BLOG PLANNER

BLOG POST 37

Blog post topic
Purpose of post
Post title ideas
Key points to include

Words and phrases to use	Keywords and Tags
Workflow Write your post on your platform Insert your links Check your spelling Insert images Add in categories and Tags Add META description and keywords Publish your post Promote on social media	Images to use
	Publish date

BLOG PLANNER

Section 1

Section 2

Section 3

Final paragraph or call to action

BLOG PLANNER

BLOG POST 38

Blog post topic
Purpose of post
Post title ideas
Key points to include

Words and phrases to use	Keywords and Tags
Workflow Write your post on your platform Insert your links Check your spelling Insert images Add in categories and Tags Add META description and keywords Publish your post Promote on social media	Images to use
	Publish date

BLOG PLANNER

Section 1

Section 2

Section 3

Final paragraph or call to action

BLOG PLANNER

BLOG POST 39

Blog post topic
Purpose of post
Post title ideas
Key points to include

Words and phrases to use	Keywords and Tags
Workflow Write your post on your platform Insert your links Check your spelling Insert images Add in categories and Tags Add META description and keywords Publish your post Promote on social media	Images to use
	Publish date

BLOG PLANNER

Section 1

Section 2

Section 3

Final paragraph or call to action

BLOG PLANNER

BLOG POST 40

Blog post topic
Purpose of post
Post title ideas
Key points to include

Words and phrases to use	Keywords and Tags
Workflow Write your post on your platform Insert your links Check your spelling Insert images Add in categories and Tags Add META description and keywords Publish your post Promote on social media	Images to use
	Publish date

BLOG PLANNER

Section 1

Section 2

Section 3

Final paragraph or call to action

BLOG PLANNER

BLOG POST 41

Blog post topic
Purpose of post
Post title ideas
Key points to include

Words and phrases to use	Keywords and Tags
Workflow Write your post on your platform Insert your links Check your spelling Insert images Add in categories and Tags Add META description and keywords Publish your post Promote on social media	Images to use
	Publish date

BLOG PLANNER

Section 1

Section 2

Section 3

Final paragraph or call to action

BLOG PLANNER

BLOG POST 42

Blog post topic
Purpose of post
Post title ideas
Key points to include

Words and phrases to use	Keywords and Tags
Workflow Write your post on your platform Insert your links Check your spelling Insert images Add in categories and Tags Add META description and keywords Publish your post Promote on social media	Images to use
	Publish date

BLOG PLANNER

Section 1

Section 2

Section 3

Final paragraph or call to action

BLOG PLANNER

BLOG POST 43

Blog post topic
Purpose of post
Post title ideas
Key points to include

Words and phrases to use	Keywords and Tags
Workflow
Write your post on your platform
Insert your links
Check your spelling
Insert images
Add in categories and Tags
Add META description and keywords
Publish your post
Promote on social media	Images to use
	Publish date

BLOG PLANNER

Section 1

Section 2

Section 3

Final paragraph or call to action

BLOG PLANNER

BLOG POST 44

Blog post topic
Purpose of post
Post title ideas
Key points to include

Words and phrases to use	Keywords and Tags
Workflow Write your post on your platform Insert your links Check your spelling Insert images Add in categories and Tags Add META description and keywords Publish your post Promote on social media	**Images to use**
	Publish date

BLOG PLANNER

Section 1

Section 2

Section 3

Final paragraph or call to action

BLOG PLANNER

BLOG POST 45

Blog post topic
Purpose of post
Post title ideas
Key points to include

Words and phrases to use	Keywords and Tags
Workflow Write your post on your platform Insert your links Check your spelling Insert images Add in categories and Tags Add META description and keywords Publish your post Promote on social media	Images to use
	Publish date

BLOG PLANNER

Section 1

Section 2

Section 3

Final paragraph or call to action

BLOG PLANNER

BLOG POST 46

Blog post topic
Purpose of post
Post title ideas
Key points to include

Words and phrases to use	Keywords and Tags
Workflow Write your post on your platform Insert your links Check your spelling Insert images Add in categories and Tags Add META description and keywords Publish your post Promote on social media	Images to use
	Publish date

www.AnchorOnline.co.uk

BLOG PLANNER

Section 1

Section 2

Section 3

Final paragraph or call to action

BLOG PLANNER

BLOG POST 47

Blog post topic

Purpose of post

Post title ideas

Key points to include

Words and phrases to use	Keywords and Tags
Workflow Write your post on your platform Insert your links Check your spelling Insert images Add in categories and Tags Add META description and keywords Publish your post Promote on social media	**Images to use**
	Publish date

BLOG PLANNER

Section 1

Section 2

Section 3

Final paragraph or call to action

BLOG PLANNER

BLOG POST 48

Blog post topic
Purpose of post
Post title ideas
Key points to include

Words and phrases to use	Keywords and Tags
Workflow Write your post on your platform Insert your links Check your spelling Insert images Add in categories and Tags Add META description and keywords Publish your post Promote on social media	Images to use
	Publish date

BLOG PLANNER

Section 1

Section 2

Section 3

Final paragraph or call to action

BLOG PLANNER

BLOG POST 49

Blog post topic
Purpose of post
Post title ideas
Key points to include

Words and phrases to use	Keywords and Tags
Workflow Write your post on your platform Insert your links Check your spelling Insert images Add in categories and Tags Add META description and keywords Publish your post Promote on social media	Images to use
	Publish date

BLOG PLANNER

Section 1

Section 2

Section 3

Final paragraph or call to action

BLOG PLANNER

BLOG POST 50

Blog post topic
Purpose of post
Post title ideas
Key points to include

Words and phrases to use	Keywords and Tags
Workflow Write your post on your platform Insert your links Check your spelling Insert images Add in categories and Tags Add META description and keywords Publish your post Promote on social media	Images to use
	Publish date

BLOG PLANNER

Section 1

Section 2

Section 3

Final paragraph or call to action

BLOG PLANNER

BLOG POST 51

Blog post topic
Purpose of post
Post title ideas
Key points to include

Words and phrases to use	Keywords and Tags
Workflow Write your post on your platform Insert your links Check your spelling Insert images Add in categories and Tags Add META description and keywords Publish your post Promote on social media	**Images to use**
	Publish date

BLOG PLANNER

Section 1

Section 2

Section 3

Final paragraph or call to action

BLOG PLANNER

BLOG POST 52

Blog post topic
Purpose of post
Post title ideas
Key points to include

Words and phrases to use	Keywords and Tags
Workflow Write your post on your platform Insert your links Check your spelling Insert images Add in categories and Tags Add META description and keywords Publish your post Promote on social media	Images to use
	Publish date

BLOG PLANNER

Section 1

Section 2

Section 3

Final paragraph or call to action

BLOG PLANNER

BLOG POST 53

Blog post topic
Purpose of post
Post title ideas
Key points to include

Words and phrases to use	Keywords and Tags
Workflow Write your post on your platform Insert your links Check your spelling Insert images Add in categories and Tags Add META description and keywords Publish your post Promote on social media	Images to use
	Publish date

BLOG PLANNER

Section 1

Section 2

Section 3

Final paragraph or call to action

BLOG PLANNER

NOTES

BLOG PLANNER

NOTES

BLOG PLANNER

NOTES

BLOG PLANNER

NOTES

BLOG PLANNER

NOTES

BLOG PLANNER

NOTES

NOTES

NOTES

NOTES

BLOG PLANNER

NOTES

BLOG PLANNER

Thank you for buying this book, I really hope it has helped with your blog planning

You can find more information over on my website www.anchoronline.co.uk and you can always join my Facebook group @anchoronlinedesigns for all of the latest updates, workshops and courses.

I would love to know how you've gotten on with this book.

You can find me on Facebook and Instagram
@anchoronlinedesigns

www.anchoronline.co.uk
laura@anchoronline.co.uk

Laura x

48876767R00069

Printed in Poland
by Amazon Fulfillment
Poland Sp. z o.o., Wrocław